A Collector's Guide to Depression Glass

The Stock Market Crash of 1929, also known as "Black Tuesday," marked the cataclysmic start of the Great Depression, the largest financial downturn in U.S. history. The widespread impact of the economic disaster led to conservative consumer behavior that lasted the next decade: only shopping for what you could afford, foregoing luxury brands, and abandoning any brand loyalties that existed before the Crash.

Despite the financial strain on consumers and businesses, a few creative glass manufacturers managed to survive by producing affordable glassware and creating effective strategies for distribution. This inexpensive glassware—commonly known as Depression glass—was mass-produced from 1920 to 1950. Today these Depression-era relics are widely collected in the United States.

A Brief History of Depression Glass

At the turn of the 20th century, hand-crafted glassware was a household staple for wealthy families. Delicate crystal plates and cups were manufactured in small shops called Hand houses, where intricate hand finishes were added to glassware. As the cost to make detailed glassware was high, hand-crafted glassware was considered a luxury item, and was only accessible to the wealthy. During the 1920s,

some glassmakers identified a need for affordable glassware to market to working class American families as a way to expand their business. Thus the production of unfinished glassware, offered at accessible price-points, began.

Manufacturing

When the Great Depression began, costly glassware fell out of favor among consumers. Depression glass grew popular among female consumers who sought the aesthetic of expensive place settings for a fraction of the cost. Over twenty manufacturers produced Depression glass from the 1920s to the 1950s, including Jeanette, Hazel Atlas, and Anchor-Hocking.

Distribution

Manufacturers optimized their production processes and were able to sell twelve-piece dinnerware sets for under two dollars. Since the manufacturing of Depression glass was relatively inexpensive, companies began offering Depression glass objects as promotional items. Glass pieces were included in cereal boxes and given away at movie theaters or gas stations to retain loyal customers during the recession. Consumers trying to save money took advantage of these promotions and slowly built complete dinnerware sets by collecting promotional goods over time.

Depression Glass Characteristics

Each manufacturer that produced Depression glass developed favored colors and shapes, as well as signature patterns — with some that were widely sold and some that were created in smaller batches. In the years that followed Depression glass production, many fake or reproduction pieces entered the market, which is why it's important for collectors to understand the characteristics of authentic Depression glass, and know what to look for.

Color

Depression glass was produced in virtually every color. Yellow and amber patterns were the popular choice for the era, followed by green, blue, pink, and crystal. Manufacturers created a few patterns in unique hues such as alexandrite and tangerine, which ultimately failed in the marketplace. In today's market, these unpopular colors are highly sought after by collectors, while the common varieties like yellow and amber have been rendered worthless.

Pattern

During the thirty years of production, over 100 patterns of Depression glass were manufactured. Each company had signature patterns, each of which are worth different amounts in the market today. Some of the most common patterns were Cameo, Mayfair, American Sweetheart, Princess, and Royal Lace. The romantic and idealistic names reflected a societal longing for the prosperity of the 1920s, a time that propagated dreams of a successful life to come.

Unique Conditions

Depression glass was produced in virtually every color. Yellow and amber patterns were the popular choice for the era, followed by green, blue, pink, and crystal. Manufacturers created a few patterns in unique hues such as alexandrite and tangerine, which ultimately failed in the marketplace. In today's market, these unpopular colors are highly sought after by collectors, while the common varieties like yellow and amber have been rendered worthless.

Tips For Collectors

While many of the common patterns in yellow or amber can be acquired for just a few dollars, patterns that were short-lived during the Great Depression are particularly valuable. Glass that was once worth less than a quarter can be worth thousands of dollars today. Whether you are just starting your collection or have had years of experience, there are a few key tips to keep in mind when buying a new piece.

One of the most challenging aspects of collecting Depression glass is finding pieces that aren't flawed. Since these glasses were made for daily use, many available pieces have years of wear on them. When examining a piece of glassware, keep an eye out for these three common condition issues:

- Cracks, scratches, and chips: A large percentage of Depression glass on the market is riddled with imperfections, which can be hard to spot from initial inspection. For scratches and cracks in the glass, it is best to hold the piece up to the light. To find chips, run your fingers along the edges and base of the glass to make sure it doesn't have any imperfections.

- Sick glass: One of the common imperfections that Depression glass features is cloudy etching caused by automatic dishwashers. Collectors refer to glass with this problem as "sick glass." When glass suffers this type of damage, it can't be restored and significantly decreases in value.

- Water rings: If the glass looks cloudy, look closely to determine if it is sick glass or simply stained with water. The latter can often be fully restored and is worth the investment.

Patterns and Popular Colors

The current collector's market is directly related to the popularity of certain patterns of glass during the Great Depression. The popular patterns and colors from the 1930s are commonly found in antique stores and auctions across the United States, but are only worth a few dollars. On the other hand, less popular patterns and colors are widely sought after.

American Sweetheart (1930–1936)

Macbeth Evans Glass Company, a prolific Depression glass manufacturer, known for their thin and delicate glass, produced a pattern called American Sweetheart that was manufactured from 1930 to 1936. American Sweetheart was produced in large quantities in the color pink. Though these pieces are common, the soft pink tone has made this pattern desirable a century later.

Cameo (1930–1934)

The Cameo pattern was the third most popular line made by Anchor Hocking Glass Company. From 1930 to 1934 it was created in green, yellow, pink, and crystal. Today, while green Cameo pieces are very common and can be purchased for just a few dollars, pink and yellow pieces are very rare due to limited production and can be worth hundreds.

Princess (1931–1934)

Anchor Hocking Glass Company, a giant in the Depression glass industry, created several patterns that were wildly popular. From 1931 to 1934 they created the Princess pattern in pink, green, and topaz. Princess pieces are treasured by collectors for their signature scalloped edges.

Mayfair (1931–1937)

Mayfair was another pattern made by Anchor Hocking Glass Company. This pattern was produced in pink, blue, yellow, and green from 1931 to 1937. In the 1930s, pink was the most popular color of the Mayfair pattern, making it a common find in today's market. Blue Mayfair pieces, however, are highly sought-after and can be worth several hundred dollars.

Royal Lace (1934–1941)

The most sought after pattern of Depression glass is arguably Royal Lace, which was made by the Hazel-Atlas Glass Company. This pattern was manufactured in green, pink, crystal, and most notably, cobalt blue. This signature blue glass was only produced from 1936 to 1941, making it more valuable than the other colored patterns of Royal Lace.

DEPRESSION GLASS
PATTERNS PRICE GUIDE

Cambridge Green Art Deco/Depression Glass Bowl - Etched Urn

1930

Cambridge Green Art Deco/Depression Glass Bowl - Etched Urn

29.99$

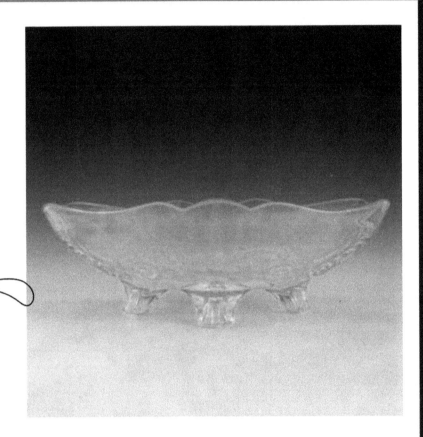

Description

A wonderful large and heavy (1.4 kilos unpacked) art deco green glass oval footed bowl, with etched urn design. Produced by American company Cambridge Glass in the 1930's, the bowl shape is pattern number '3400/1240', and the etched design seems to be a variation of pattern number '739'.

Size

Measures approx 4 inches tall by 12.75 inches in diameter at widest point.

Condition

Excellent condition, no chips or cracks.

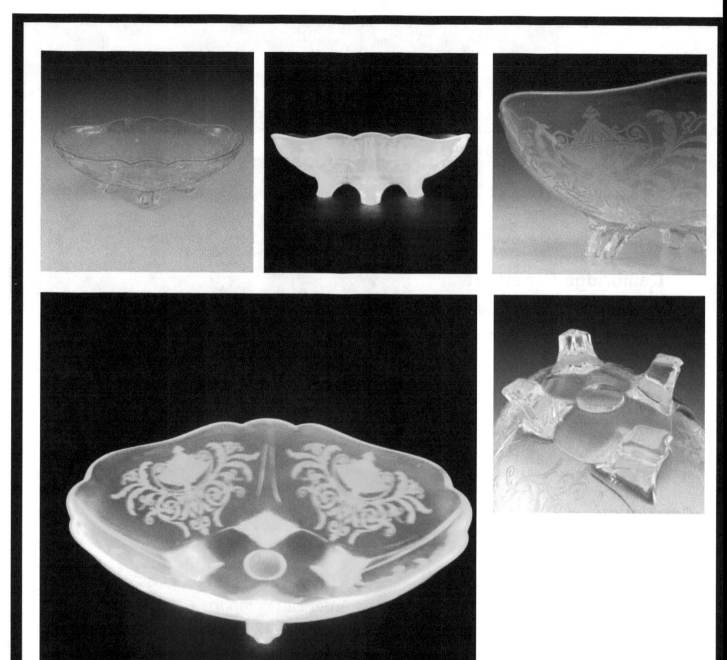

Hazel Atlas Royal Lace Depression Glass Sugar Bowl

1930

Hazel Atlas Royal Lace Depression Glass Sugar Bowl

24.99$

Description

Here is a 1930's American depression glass sugar bowl, from Hazel Atlas, part of their "Royal Lace" range. Made in vaseline/uranium green glass, which glows brightly in UV light.

Size

Measures approx 4.25 inches tall by 5.25 inches in diameter at widest point.

Condition

Excellent condition, no chips or cracks.

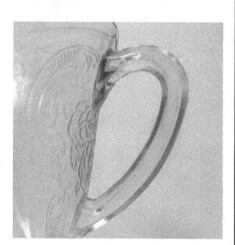

Hazel Atlas Royal Lace Pink Depression Glass Vintage Sugar Bowl

1930

Hazel Atlas Royal Lace Pink Depression Glass Vintage Sugar Bowl

32.99$

Description

A 1930's American Depression era pink glass open sugar bowl, from Hazel Atlas, part of their "Royal Lace" pattern range.

Size

Measures approx 4 inches tall by 5.25 inches in diameter at widest point.**Condition**

Excellent condition, no chips or cracks.

1930

Jeannette Poinsettia Floral Depression Glass Plate

22.49$

Description

A 1930's American depression glass plate from the Jeannette Glass Company, part of their "Poinsettia" (Floral) range. Made in vaseline/uranium green glass, which glows brightly in UV light! A must for any collection.

Size

Measures approx 4 inches tall by 5.25 inches in diameter at widest point.

Condition

Excellent condition, no chips or cracks.

Jeannette Poinsettia Floral Depression Glass Tumbler

1930

Jeannette Poinsettia Floral Depression Glass Tumbler

19.99$

Description

Here is a 1930's American depression glass footed tumbler from the Jeannette Glass Company, part of their "Poinsettia" (Floral) range. Made in vaseline/uranium green glass, which glows brightly in UV light.

Size

Measures approx 4 inches tall by 3 inches in diameter at widest point.

Condition

Excellent condition, no chips or cracks.

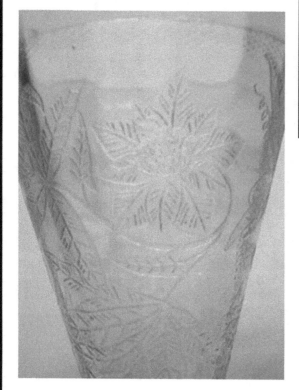

Jeannette Poinsettia Floral Green Depression Glass Bowl

1930

Jeannette Poinsettia Floral Green Depression Glass Bowl

26.99$

Description

Here is a 1930's American depression glass lidded sugar bowl from the Jeannette Glass Company, part of their "Poinsettia" (Floral) range. Made in vaseline/uranium green glass, which glows brightly in UV light.

Size

Measures approx 5 inches tall by 5.5 inches in diameter at widest point.

Condition

Excellent condition, no chips or cracks.

Jeannette Poinsettia Floral Green Depression Glass Bowl

1930

Jeannette Poinsettia Floral Green Depression Glass Bowl

22.99$

Description

Here is a 1930's American depression glass bowl from the Jeannette Glass Company, part of their "Poinsettia" (Floral) range. Made in vaseline/uranium green glass, which glows brightly in UV light.

Size

Measures approx 3 inches tall by 7.5 inches in diameter at widest point.

Condition

Excellent condition, no chips or cracks.

Jeannette Poinsettia Floral Green Depression Glass Dish

1930

Jeannette Poinsettia Floral Green Depression Glass Dish

24.99$

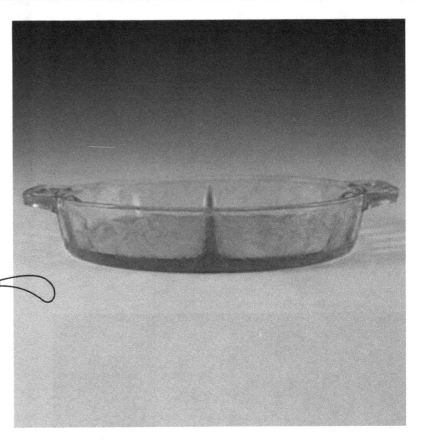

Description

Here is a 1930's American depression glass dish/nibbles tray from the Jeannette Glass Company, part of their "Poinsettia" (Floral) range. Made in vaseline/uranium green glass, which glows brightly in UV light! A must for any collection.

Size

Measures approx 1.25 inches tall by 8.25 inches in diameter at widest point.

Condition

Excellent condition, no chips or cracks.

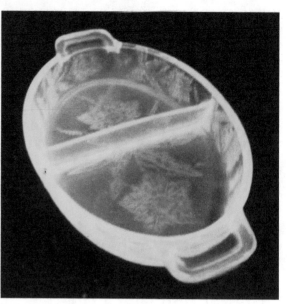

Jeannette Poinsettia Floral Green Depression Glass Jug/Pitcher

1930

Jeannette Poinsettia Floral Green Depression Glass Jug/Pitcher

33.99$

Description

Here is a very rare 1930's American depression glass jug/pitcher from the Jeannette Glass Company, part of their "Poinsettia" (Floral) range. Made in uranium green glass, which glows brightly in UV light.

Size

Measures approx 1.25 inches tall by 8.25 inches in diameter at widest point.

Condition

Excellent condition, no chips or cracks, other than a small nick to the spout part of the rim, and a couple of small nicks to the base rim. There is also a couple of manufacturing "straw marks" to the side near the handle. All shown in final pictures. Please note: straw marks can look and even feel a bit like cracks if you are not used to seeing them, but they are very common in depression glass and other pressed glassware, caused when a section of hot molten glass is cut with scissors during the manufacturing process

Jeannette Poinsettia Floral Green Depression Glass Vase

1930

Jeannette Poinsettia Floral Green Depression Glass Vase

27.49$

Description

Here is a very rare 1930's American depression glass vase from the Jeannette Glass Company, part of their "Poinsettia" (Floral) range. Made in uranium green glass, which glows brightly in UV light.

Size

Measures approx 6.75 inches tall by 4.25 inches in diameter at widest point.

Condition

Excellent condition, no chips or cracks,

Large Hazel Atlas Royal Lace Pink Depression Glass Bowl

1930

Large Hazel Atlas Royal Lace Pink Depression Glass Bowl

34.99$

Description

Here is a large 1930's American pink depression glass bowl, from Hazel Atlas, part of their "Royal Lace" range.

Size

Measures approx 4.25 inches tall by 10 inches in diameter at widest point.

Condition

Excellent condition, no chips or cracks,

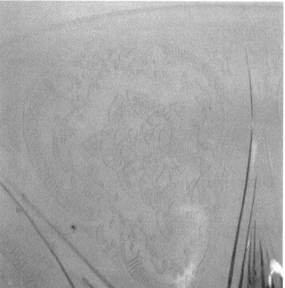

Adam Pink Depression Glass Cup

1934

Adam Pink Depression Glass Cup

18.99$

Description

Jeannette's Adam is popular and some pieces are hard to find. You can assemble a complete dinner set plus candle holders, candy dish, vase. The accessory pieces tend to be expensive. You'll want to watch for damage on the inner rims as they tend to get nicked. Adam has not been reproduced.

Colors: Mostly pink and green with a few pieces of translucent Delphite blue, yellow and crystal.

Adam's Rib Pink Depression Glass Covered Candy Jar

1925

Adam's Rib Pink Depression Glass Covered Candy Jar

38.99$

Description

Adams Rib is not well known which is a shame since it has a refined elegant look. The design is narrow ribs with smooth bands near the rim. It mostly came in accessory pieces, like the candy jar shown, plus you can collect a small lunch set.

Colors: Mostly pink and green with a few pieces of translucent Delphite blue, yellow and crystal.

1936

American Sweetheart Depression Glass

22.99$

Description

American Sweetheart is one of the most beloved patterns and you can readily find most pieces. You can get a complete dinner set without spending a fortune. Some serving pieces, like the sugar lid, tumblers and cream soups are pricey but you don't have to get them.

The monax white is elegant and ethereal, an excellent choice even if you don't ordinarily care for white glass. It is translucent and so thin that some pieces have a blue tinge on the rims.

Colors: Pink and translucent monax white. There are a few cobalt blue and red pieces and some monax has gold or colored trim on the rim

1920

Aunt Polly Depression Glass

124.99$

Description

Aunt Polly suffers from not being well known and it has rough seams, which is typical of US Glass. The blue is quite pretty.

1930

Aurora Depression Glass

22.99$

Description

Aurora is stunning in blue. There are not a lot of pieces available, just a cup and saucer, two bowls, small plate and the tumbler shown. It works well mixed with other patterns. It would be fun to create a set of blue depression glass that mixed different patterns together. Hazel Atlas made Aurora, Moderntone, Newport and New Century, which are among the more common blue depression glass, so all these patterns are the same color and blend well together.

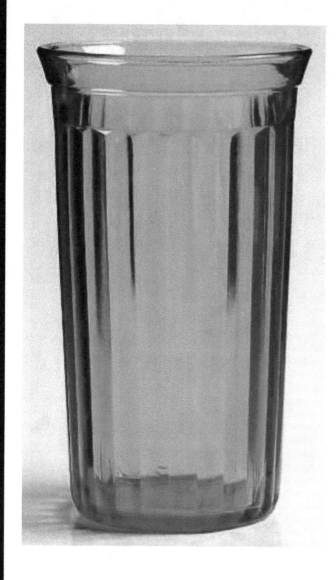

1933

**Block Optic
Depression Glass**

39.99$

Description

Block Optic is the old reliable in depression glass. You will find some at almost every antique store and the range of pieces is astonishing. There are at least 5 different creamers and sugars and cups, multiple tumblers, sherbets and goblets, plus a full dinnerware set and many accessory pieces. The green seems the most prevalent followed by yellow, at least in mid-Michigan.

If you are looking for a fun pattern to collect then choose Block Optic. It is pretty, displays beautifully in a cupboard or on the table, reasonably priced and fun to find.

1920

Bowknot Depression Glass

51.99$

Description

Bowknot is very pretty with mold etched design of ribbon all tied in bows with swags between. There are only a few pieces, tumblers, small plate and bowls, sherbet and cup.

1934

Cameo Depression Glass

64.99$

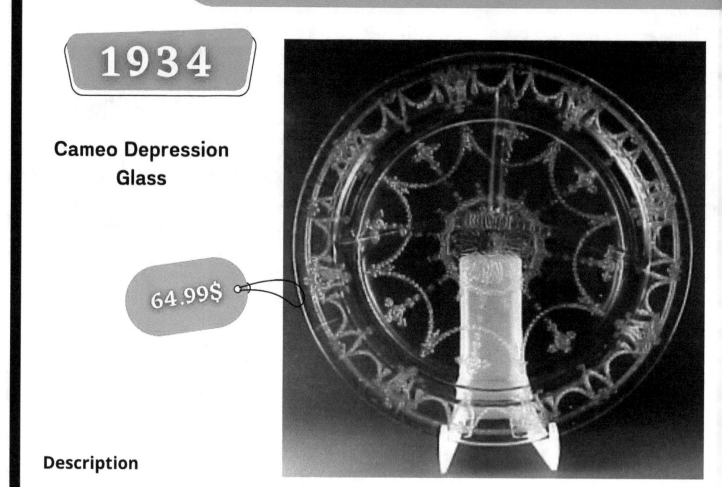

Description

Cameo is another Hocking pattern with tons of pieces to choose, including stemware, tumblers, accessory pieces and a full dinner set. The pattern has a dancer draped in scarves, likely Isidore Duncan, in small cameos around the rim connected with swags and flowers. The design was modified from Monongah's Springtime plate etching to allow the Cameo pattern to be mass produced.

Shakers have been reproduced in different colors than the originals and Mosser Glass made a line of small children's dishes called "Jennifer" that you may see advertised to go with American Girl dolls. These reproductions and remakes are easy to tell so you should not worry about being fooled.

This is a gorgeous pattern, one of the prettiest depression glass and you won't go wrong with it. We specialize in Cameo depression glass listed here.

Cherry Blossom Depression Glass

1939

Cherry Blossom Depression Glass

Description

Cherry Blossom is one of the most lovely depression glass patterns. Sadly many piece have been reproduced, notably cups, saucers, dinner plates, small bowls, butter dishes, tumblers, pitchers and shakers. Most of the fakes have tell-tale faults. If you like Cherry Blossom I recommend you get at least one good depression glass book and learn about the fakes. Gene Florence's Collector s Encyclopedia of Depression Glass,19th Edition (Collector's Encyclopedia of Depression Glass) is good.

Chinex and Cremax Depression Glass

1941

Chinex and Cremax Depression Glass

25.99$

Description

MacBeth Evans made several variations of translucent creamy colored glass with different rim designs and decorations. The one shown is Cremax with a brown castle scene.

1934

Colonial Knife and Fork Depression Glass

22.99$

Description

Colonial can be fun to collect with the many pieces including stemware, tumblers, bowls, dinnerware and pitchers.

1934

Columbia
Depression Glass

22.99$

Description

Columbia is heavy with a solid design of molded rays and inset dots. It sparkles in the light.

1933

Cube Cubist Depression Glass

09.99$

Description

People mistake Cube for Fostoria's American pattern and the knock off of American, Whitehall. If you find amber or olive green they are Whitehall. Pink or clear could be Cube but it would be good to get a book that shows Cube and get familiar with the pieces. This is another pattern where if you get familiar with the glass you won't have any problem with reproductions or similar patterns.

1941

Diana Depression Glass

12.99$

Description

Isn't this demitasse set pretty with the platinum trim on clear depression glass? The cup and saucer are small and have the narrow swirled ribs we find in Diana.

1932

Dogwood Depression Glass

12.99$

Description

Dogwood is drop dead gorgeous. The glass is thin, which we find in other MacBeth Evans patterns, and the pattern is all over big flowers. It looks like a brocade. You can find most pieces – a small dinner set and even some tumblers – fairly reasonably priced. There are a couple pieces that are expensive, like the pitcher. Dogwood doesn't seem too prone to damage, a good thing. There are enough pieces you can have fun with it. We specialize in Dogwood and have pieces here.

1938

Doric Depression Glass

15.99$

Description

Doric is pretty and there are enough pieces to make it fun to collect. Most pieces are moderately priced. There is a band of three narrow ridges just below the pattern band on most pieces. You'll want to check those ridges carefully for little nicks.

1938

Doric and Pansy Depression Glass

11.99$

Description

Doric and Pansy is a little busier than Doric since the squares that are plain in Doric are filled with a pansy flower in Doric and Pansy. Jeannette made a child's set too, which is called Pretty Polly.

1935

Floragold Louisa Depression Glass

08.99$

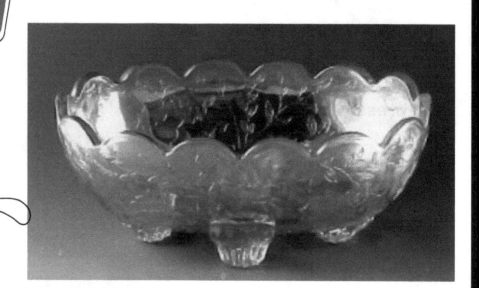

Description

Strictly speaking Floragold is not true depression glass because it was made in the 1950s, but the pattern and styling is so typical of the depression era that collectors commonly consider it with depression glass. Most pieces are square and there are many to choose among.

1935

Floral Poinsettia Depression Glass

17.99$

Description

Floral or Poinsettia is one of the patterns we carry here. It has big exuberant flowers and leaves all over and comes in a beautiful array of pieces. The only pieces that have been reproduced are the shakers.

Supposedly the flowers on Floral are poinsettias, but the leaves look nothing like poinsettias – and the flowers look more like passion flowers. Remember that back in the 1930s, when Floral came out, poinsettias were exotic flowers, not the ubiquitous Christmas plants we all know today.

1938

Fortune Depression Glass

15.99$

Description

Fortune is a pretty pattern that has only a few pieces, enough to set the table for lunch. Sometimes people confuse Fortune with Old Cafe. You can tell Fortune because it has one wide panel alternating with one narrow panel.

Georgian Lovebirds Depression Glass

1936

**Georgian Lovebirds
Depression Glass**

17.99$

Description

Georgian Lovebirds is one of my favorite patterns. There are triangular motifs that alternate two birds with a basket of flowers and all are connected by swags and a molded band. Georgian has a nice assortment of pieces and is moderately priced. Yes, you can spend a lot on a few rare pieces but you can get everything you need without too much difficulty.

You may find statements on the internet that any unmarked Georgian is a reproduction. This is not true. Green Georgian has not been reproduced. Some cups, saucers and sherbets are marked but most are not. The markings have more to do with the exact production date since Federal marked only some glass.

1949

Holiday Buttons and Bows Depression Glass

21.99$

Description

Jeannette's Holiday is not truly depression glass since it was made in the 1940s but it slips in based on the colors and the style. It's a molded design with lots of surface texture. The pink is a lovely clear color.

1932

**Iris and Herringbone
Depression Glass**

20.99$

Description

Iris is a neat pattern that has a background like a herringbone tweed and big iris flowers and leaves in relief on top. This pattern pops in iridescent and sparkles in the clear.

Jeannette made a lot of interesting pieces and most are reasonably available and in the moderately expensive range. It's odd but tumblers are some of the easiest pieces to find and are inexpensive.

There have been a few pieces reproduced which are supposed to be easy to tell. If you like Iris then I highly recommend the book Collector s Encyclopedia of Depression Glass,19th Edition (Collector's Encyclopedia of Depression Glass)

by Gene Florence which has a thorough description of the fakes.

Lorain Basket Depression Glass

1932

Lorain Basket Depression Glass

24.99$

Description

Lorain is incredible, very lovely in both green and yellow. It looks wonderful on a table and having even a few pieces will add style and color. Most pieces are square. Plates have the baskets on the corners with swags on the sides and big medallions in the centers.

The only point against Lorain is the seams are usually raised enough that you can feel them.

Here is a link to a tablescape we did with all Lorain green depression glass, and just one picture from that to give you an idea how gorgeous this glass is. Here are our Lorain pieces in stock.

1943

Manhattan Depression Glass

21.99$

Description

You can get a small dinner set in Manhattan but the pieces that have the most looks are the accessories like the tilt pitcher, vase, candy jar and relish tray.

Mayfair Open Rose Depression Glass

1937

Mayfair Open Rose Depression Glass

33.99$

Description

You can get a full dinner set in Mayfair plus goblets, tumblers, accessory pieces and many bowls and decorative pieces. About the only piece Hocking did not make in Mayfair was a candle holder.

Like Block Optic, Mayfair is a collectors dream. There are so many pieces to choose among, the pattern is lovely, colors are super. You can get a nice collection without spending a fortune as the basic pieces are moderately priced, especially in pink. There are a few rare pieces that serious collectors chase that are expensive and color plays a big role in price.

Mayfair doesn't seem particularly prone to damage. Although plates have rims the interior edge is rounded which helps a lot to reduce damage.

Miss America Depression Glass

1938

Miss America Depression Glass

69.99$

Description

Miss America remains one of the most popular patterns. It is sparkly and pretty and has a lot of looks in any of the colors. Miss America footed pieces have square bottoms and plates have molded stars in the center and wide rims with diamond shapes on the back.

Miss America was one of the patterns people used for their good dishes. It looks fancy.

You can easily get a set in clear quite inexpensively. Pink is more costly but you'll find most pieces are still affordable and can be found. Please be sure to check for surface wear and nicks on the points. Also be aware that the smooth rims can get clunked and damaged if people are careless.

1942

Moderntone Depression Glass

14.99$

Description

If you love blue then you can't go wrong with Moderntone. There are a lot pieces to choose among and you can get a dinner set and serving pieces quite easily and at moderate expense.

The only thing you have to be careful of with Moderntone is surface wear. This may not matter to you if you intend to use your glass for meals. If it does matter then be sure to hold plates up to the light and check for scratches and haziness.

Moderntone has the classic good looks of Art Deco – and those rings look a little outer space.

Hazel Atlas re-issued Moderntone in platonite white glass with fired on colors in the 1950s. You can find a rainbow of colors.

1940

Newport Hairpin Depression Glass

14.99$

Description

Newport is one of the easiest depression patterns to find in amethyst glass. It's a prettier shade than the photo shows with more life. Early collectors nicknamed this Hairpin for the scallop lines.

Hazel Atlas reused the pattern blanks to make white platonite with fired on colors after the depression.

1940

**Normandie
Depression
Glass**

17.99$

Description

Normandie is an exceptionally pretty pattern with bouquets between trellis like lattices. I've a soft spot for Normandie because the first piece of depression glass I bought was a Normandie dinner plate. You can get a set in amber, iridescent or pink inexpensively. Amber is more common than pink. Federal made the iridescent after the depression era; it is a dark marigold color.

Horseshoe Depression Glass

1940

Horseshoe Depression Glass

19.99$

Description

Indiana Glass gave this pattern the exciting name of Number 612 but a much better name is Horseshoe. The design has big horseshoe shaped motifs with lots of flowers, very pretty. Some pieces have raised seams which is common with Indiana depression glass.

You can bet a nice set for lunch or dinner with tumblers and accessory pieces. Horseshoe is moderately expensive and not as plentiful as some.

1932

Vernon Depression Glass

13.99$

Description

Vernon is pretty but not there were only a few pieces made. You could serve lunch with Vernon. It is not terribly common yet it is inexpensive. Pieces have raised seams which is common with Indiana depression glass.

1937

Pineapple and Floral Depression Glass

27.99$

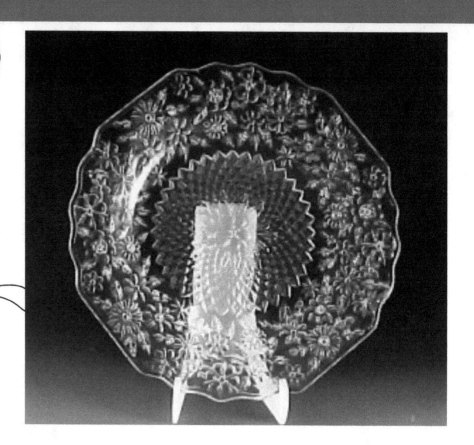

Description

Pineapple and Floral sparkles in the light and has a pretty design. Pieces have raised seams.

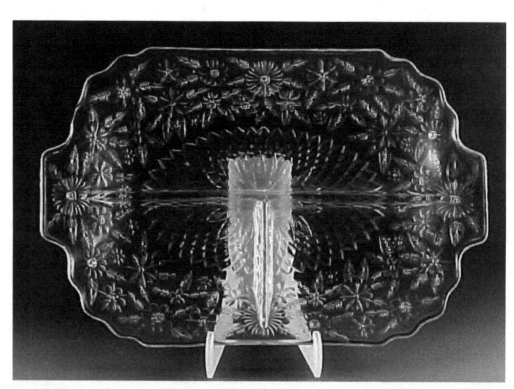

1940

Old Cafe Depression Glass

23.99$

Description

You can get a dinner set but the accessory and pieces like the candy dish and olive dish are more interesting. Old Cafe has two narrow panels between one wider panel.

1938

Old Colony Depression Glass

31.99$

Description

You can get a dinner set but the accessory and pieces like the candy dish and olive dish are more interesting.
Old Cafe has two narrow panels between one wider panel.

1920

Old English Depression Glass

49.99$

Description

Old English is an accessory pattern. It has no cup and saucer. Instead it has fanciful vases, compotes (Indiana's word for comport), bowls, snack plates. Pieces are finished better than the later depression glass from Indiana.

Printed in the USA
CPSIA information can be obtained
at www.ICGtesting.com
LVHW081133051223
765741LV00017B/789